Running Records
for Classroom Teachers

MARIE M. CLAY

SECOND EDITION

The Marie Clay
Literacy Trust

Running Records for Classroom Teachers
Second Edition

Photography: Christine Boocock

Cover design: Suzanne Heiser, Heinemann

Text design: Cheryl Smith, Macarn Design

© 2017 The Marie Clay Literacy Trust
Global Education Systems [GES] Ltd
5/32 St Stephens Avenue, Parnell, Auckland 1052, New Zealand
ISBN NZ 978-1-927293-09-6
ISBN USA 978-0-325-09279-9
ISBN UK 978-140717511-9

Distributed by:

Australia: Scholastic Australia Pty Ltd, PO Box 579, Gosford, NSW 2250
ABN 11 000 614 577
www.scholastic.com.au

New Zealand: Scholastic New Zealand Ltd, Private Bag 94407, Botany, Auckland 2163
www. scholastic.co.nz

UK and Eire: Scholastic Ltd, Book End, Range Road, Witney, Oxfordshire OX29 0YD
www.scholastic.co.uk/marieclay

United States: Heinemann, 361 Hanover Street, Portsmouth, NH 03801-3912
www.heinemann.com

The pronouns 'she' and 'he' have been used in this text to refer to the teacher and the child respectively. Despite a possible charge of sexist bias it makes for clearer, easier reading if such references are consistent.

Printed in China

Contents

Introduction

Records of children reading continuous text provide different kinds of information from tests of letters, sounds and words in isolation. Running Records were developed for a longitudinal research study of early literacy learning and were first published in *The Early Detection of Reading Difficulties: A Diagnostic Survey* (Clay, 1972). The procedures described in this book match the most recent description of Running Records in *An Observation Survey of Early Literacy Achievement* (Clay, 2013).

Running Records for Classroom Teachers describes some of the key ideas about using Running Records as an assessment of text reading. It introduces how to take and score a reliable record, and how that record can be interpreted. Standard ways of recording are recommended to take care of almost all the unusual behaviours teachers might encounter. The conventions described have been widely used with children who are reading English. The recording is easy for teachers to use and has proved to be a valid form of assessment.

Teachers may have to learn some new terms and concepts in order to interpret their Running Records. The procedures are simple, yet what those teachers record can challenge them to think with greater clarity about the progress of beginning readers.

Running Records are not limited to a particular theory of literacy learning. However, in any interpretation of the record, the teacher's theory of literacy learning begins to become involved. (This is discussed on pages 27–28 and 30–31.) More extended discussion of literacy learning theories associated with using and interpreting Running Records can be found in *An Observation Survey of Early Literacy Achievement* (Clay, 2013), *Becoming Literate: The Construction of Inner Control* (Clay, 2015), and *By Different Paths to Common Outcomes* (Clay, 2014).

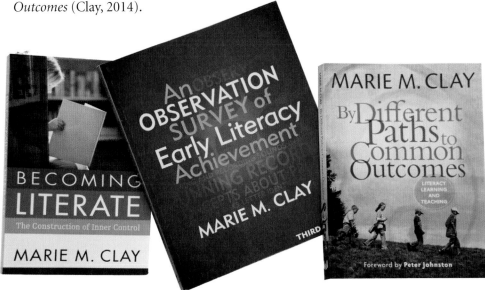

Reading continuous text

Running Records are designed to be taken as a child reads orally from any text. The successful early learner brings his speech to bear on the interpretation of print. His vocabulary, sentence patterns and pronunciation of words provide him with information that guides his identification of printed words.

The young reader learns to follow the directional conventions of written language. Until he learns something about how his eyes should scan the print, he is unlikely to make much progress with trying to read. Gradually the successful learner begins to move his eyes across the lines and over the page, searching for things he can recognise. He becomes attentive to the visual detail of words, to the spaces, the letters and the sounds that are represented. At the same time he begins to pull more than one kind of information into the seemingly simple act of reading. This early phase in learning to read can be understood as building up several layers of knowledge that are the foundation of subsequent success.

Children's progress in learning to read is often measured by testing the number of letters, or sounds, or words they know. Yet most of the time in classrooms they are engaging in reading continuous texts. They are asked to put together the messages transmitted by the letters, sounds or words.

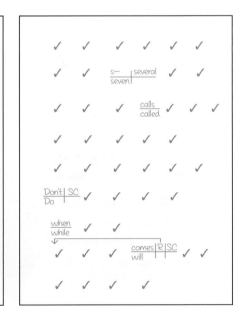

If Running Records are taken in a systematic way they provide evidence of how well children are learning to direct their knowledge of letters, sounds and words to understanding the messages in the text.

The example from a child's reading of *The Wolf and the Seven Little Kids* on the previous page explains the recording task. Look at the difficulty of the text. Count the child's errors and self-corrections (SC). Think about the things that challenged this child, the substitutions he made, and what made him correct the final substitution. The record provides evidence of the kinds of things that this child can do with the information he can get from print.

Uses for Running Records

Records are taken to guide teaching

Running Records capture what young readers say and do while reading continuous text, usually short stories or books. Having taken the record teachers can review what happened immediately, leading to teaching decisions on the spot, or at a later time as they plan for next lessons. They can judge what the reader already knows, what he attended to, and what he overlooked. They can assess how well each reader is pulling together what he knows about letters, sounds and words in order to get to the messages. This kind of information allows teachers to prompt, support and challenge individual learners. Such records allow teachers to describe how children are working on a text.

Records are taken to assess text difficulty

Running Records can be used to check on whether students are working on material of appropriate difficulty, neither too difficult nor too easy but offering a suitable level of challenge to the learner.

Records are taken to capture progress

Running Records taken at selected intervals, from the time a child tries to retell a story from the pictures in a book until he has become a silent reader, enable us to plot his path of progress in literacy learning. As teachers try to interpret each Running Record, they take into account the difficulty level of the text and make sound judgements about the reader's progress up through a gradient of difficulty in the reading books. A desirable path of progress shows that learners are meeting the challenges of reading increasingly difficult texts.

The examples in this book are selected to demonstrate how Running Records can be taken on both simple and more advanced texts. (A Running Record sheet is on page 43.)

Compare two Running Records on the same text

The following example demonstrates what a teacher could learn from Running Records. Peter and John read the same text, with the same level of accuracy but the records show that they need different emphases in their instruction.

Peter's record

The Bicycle — Title	Accuracy 85.5%	Count		Analysis of Errors and Self-corrections — Information used	
		E	SC	E MSV	SC MSV
✓ ✓ ✓ ✓					
✓ ✓ lake/lady ✓ ✓		I		M (S) (V)	
✓ ✓ box/boy ✓ ✓		I		M (S) (V)	
✓ ✓ ✓ ✓ ✓					
✓ ✓ ✓ ✓ ✓					
✓ ✓ bil/bicycle ✓		I		M S (V)	
square/squashed		I		M (S) (V)	

Peter used some visual information from the print and seemed to be paying some attention to sentence structure because his errors usually belonged to a class of words that could occur in the sentence up to the error. He did not react to the lack of meaning in what he said.

John's record

The Bicycle — Title	Accuracy 85.5%	Count		Analysis of Errors and Self-corrections — Information used	
		E	SC	E MSV	SC MSV
✓ ✓ ✓ ✓					
✓ ✓ girl/lady ✓ ✓		I		(M) (S) V	
✓ ✓ man/boy ✓ ✓		I		(M) (S) V	
✓ ✓ ✓ ✓ ✓					
✓ ✓ ✓ ✓ ✓					
✓ ✓ bike/bicycle ✓		I		(M) (S) (V)	
flat/squashed		I		(M) (S) V	

John used language information and all his errors reflected the use of meaning and sentence structure. He did not seem to be aware of the mismatch between what he said and the visual information in the text.

These examples show that Running Records can capture how beginning readers are putting together what they know in order to read text. We may question the quality of the text but it did reveal how these two children were working in different ways on the same book.

The Bicycle

The clown got on

and the lady got on

and the boy got on

and the girl got on

and the bear got on

and the bicycle got . . .

squashed.

2

Learning to take a Running Record

In every sense this activity of taking Running Records should be as relaxed as sharing a book with a child. Invite the child to read to you and tell him that you will be writing down some things. This gives him a little warning that for the next few minutes you are not going to teach. Teachers who have practised with a wide variety of children and are at ease in taking Running Records will get the most informative records and will make the fairest interpretations.

About three workshop training sessions with a professional who is very familiar with Running Records are recommended for teachers before they begin to use this as an assessment technique. It takes more than self-teaching from an instructional guide to achieve a high standard of observing, recording and interpreting. Children do unusual things, so further discussions with colleagues should be arranged. From time to time school teams should schedule monitoring sessions to review whether the recording and interpretation of Running Records is being conducted with consistency.

What does skilled record-taking look like?

A classroom teacher should, ideally, be able to sit down beside a child with a blank sheet of paper and take a Running Record when the moment is right. Teachers should practise until it is as easy as that. Any text, at any time, as and when appropriate, should be the aim. Then this technique will be flexible enough to suit any classroom conditions. It will also be more likely that the teacher's record can be relied upon to be an accurate account. (See page 6 for a short example.)

Teachers should prepare themselves to get the record down while the child is reading. At first, the easy-to-notice things are recorded. Over time it becomes easy to record more. When they can record the essentials, teachers find that they can note also what the child said about the task, or how he moved across print, or which hand he used to point, and other interesting things like turning back several pages and correcting an earlier error. With practice, teachers get more information from their observations and records.

At first, the task seems to require the recorder's full attention without interruption but before long teachers become bold enough to work in a busy classroom. The class comes to accept that the taking of Running Records is common practice and they will leave the teacher alone to get the job done.

Teachers should learn to take Running Records in ways that will allow them to use this technique with standard administration, recording and interpretation.

Two things to avoid

Pre-printed recording sheets There is not enough room on a pre-printed page of text for the teacher to record all the unusual things that can occur. Many teachers are surprised to find that a printed text often will not allow all of the child's behaviours to be recorded. This is because a Running Record is not just about right or wrong words. It is about a lot more than that. Beginning readers do not keep closely to the text; they sometimes leave out large sections and insert things that are not there; they change direction, go back over what they have read, and confuse themselves.

A Running Record needs to capture all the behaviour that helps us to interpret what the child was probably doing. Everything the child said and did tells us something; when the reading is correct, what his hands and eyes were doing, the comments he made, when he repeated a line of text, and so on. After a Running Record a teacher should be able to 'hear' the reading again when reviewing the record. This is the aim.

Limiting observations to a few select texts, pre-printed on a scoring sheet, will provide less useful information. Young readers do very interesting things as they attempt to get an acceptable message from the pages of a book, and the object of Running Records is to get valid records of how children are arriving at their decisions. Authors and publishers try to make it easy for teachers by providing pre-printed texts but children's problem-solving on texts is too diverse to conform to a published layout. A printed text encourages teachers to attend only to right and wrong responses, and *to ignore how the child is arriving at these decisions.*

Voice recording Avoid the use of a voice recorder. Having to record the assessment is an aid to get rid of as soon as possible, so why not start without it? Voice recording may seem easier at first, but it limits the analysis because only sounds and language are recorded. It provides no information about how the child moved, seemed puzzled, peered at the print or looked at the ceiling. Observations like those are helpful for understanding what young learners are trying to do.

Select children who will make practising easier

Practise on a range of readers who are about one year into school, as many as you can. Avoid practising on higher or lower progress readers until you become skilful. Good readers go too fast, and struggling readers produce complex records. For each child make records of two or three little books, or text pieces, with about 100–200 words in each, and have the child read each whole story or text. At the early reading level when the child is reading the simplest books, the numbers of words may fall below 100, but if three texts are read this will be satisfactory even though the extracts themselves are short. Once a teacher knows how to take Running Records it should take about 10 minutes to get three samples. Sharing your early records with a colleague who uses them a lot will produce useful discussions.

Select texts for practising

Any texts can be used for Running Records — books, stories, information texts, or children's published writing — but a good place to start is with a familiar text that the child has read once or twice before. This *seen* text will provide evidence of how the reader is bringing different processes and skills together. It is a good idea to start each observation with a text that is familiar to him. A book that is easy for the child will also be easy for teachers to record as they rehearse their recording techniques. *The prime purpose of a Running Record is to understand more about how children are using what they know to get to the messages of the text, or in other words what reading processes they are using.*

The teacher may want to know how the child performs on a challenging text. Sometimes she discovers that the child can work at a higher level than she anticipated. A challenging text could show whether the reader recognises the need for problem-solving and what kinds of problem-solving he tries. However, if the challenges are too great the record will not show how the reading process comes together, only how and when it falls apart.

Older proficient readers become fast readers, too fast for the teacher to make ticks (checks) for every word. Then the observer can give up recording the correct responding, and, keeping strictly to the layout and lines of the text, record everything the reader does to monitor, solve words and self-correct. This is a compromise made only for very fast readers. The record needs to be analysed immediately as it is hard to recapture the reading from such a limited record.

Finding an instructional text level

When a child reads a text with between 90 and 94 percent accuracy, this is called an instructional level because it indicates an appropriate level for the child to learn from. The record will contain some error that provides evidence of processing the information in print. Teachers can then observe how children work at monitoring their own reading. Listening to a young reader we can hear and record how the child is attending to print but as readers become proficient more of the processing is hidden from view, worked out in the child's head before a response is made.

Three levels of text difficulty

Research shows that children's learning is helped when we give them material at their personal instructional level. Recording their performance at three levels of text difficulty

> an easy text (95 to 100 percent accuracy)
> an instructional text (90 to 94 percent accuracy), and
> a hard text (80 to 89 percent accuracy)

is the most reliable way to establish what level of text should be used for instruction.

When a gradient of difficulty in text level is being used, the highest-level text the child can read with 90 percent accuracy or above indicates the instructional level. This means that to obtain an instructional level it is necessary to record the child reading a text below 90 percent accuracy (that is, a text that is hard for him).

The terms easy, instructional and hard used in relation to Running Records do not refer to the characteristics of the text itself. *They describe how a particular child read the text.* The terms do not say anything about how another child will read that text. Whether it is easy or instructional or difficult is determined entirely by how well this child was able to work on it.

When publishers suggest some order of difficulty in their books they are usually estimating how 'children in general' might find these books. Look for evidence of whether the publishers trialled their books on a sample of children and whether those children were anything like the children you teach.

For important educational decisions, it is not enough for teachers to assess children only on their current reading books. A text at each of the easy, instructional or hard levels will provide the necessary evidence for a concise summary of where that child is in his learning. (Record the text level on each Running Record sheet.) This more careful approach should be used for important educational decisions like

- moving children to groups for instruction
- observing children with particular difficulties
- selecting children for special and supplementary assistance
- making decisions about promotion, or
- carrying out a school survey of achievement.

For research studies, three levels of difficulty *must* be obtained to ensure that the assessments are reliable.

3

Taking Running Records

The following record of a book read well provides an illustration of many but not all of the recording techniques. The record must mimic the layout of lines in the text the child is reading.

"A bee!" said Baby Bear.	✓ ✓ ✓ ✓ ✓
"Where is he going?"	✓ ✓ ✓ ✓
The bee went into a tree.	✓ ✓ ✓ ✓ ✓ bush | R | SC
	tree | |
Baby Bear looked in the tree.	✓ ✓ looks | SC ✓ a | R | SC ✓
	looked | the | |
"Honey!" said Baby Bear.	✓ ✓ ✓ ✓
"Honey for me! Thank you, bee."	✓ ✓ ✓ ✓ ✓ ✓

Some observers find that entering the full stops (periods) helps them keep track of the recording and scoring.

"Honey!" said Baby Bear.	✓ ✓ ✓ ✓ .
"Honey for me! Thank you, bee."	✓ ✓ ✓ ✓ ✓ ✓ .

However, there are problems when teachers try to record pausing and phrasing because teachers' practices then tend to be unreliable.

Standard ways of recording are recommended to take care of almost all the unusual behaviours teachers might encounter. The conventions described have been widely used with children who are reading English. The recording is easy for teachers to use and is also reliable as an assessment. Running Records are not limited to a particular theory of literacy learning. However, in any interpretation of the record, the teacher's theory of literacy learning begins to become involved. (This is discussed on pages 30–31.)

Why use standard procedures?

Teachers want to be able to compare Running Records one with another. Either they want to know how Alex's record today compares with his earlier records, or they need to make some teaching decisions about several children and to compare one reader with another. The aim is to take a full record, capturing behaviour and scoring it reliably, so comparisons can be made. To make such comparisons, teachers need to have a common standard for taking records, for describing what they observe, for calculating the scores and interpreting the record.

To support the interpretation of the record, teachers should also try to write down the comments a child makes as he reads the book; working out loud, talking to himself, being surprised, giving some rationale for what he did, and any personal reactions.

Conventions for recording

1   Mark every word read correctly with a tick (or check).
    A record of the first five pages of *Early in the Morning* that had 100 percent accuracy would look like this. (The lines indicate page breaks.)

Bill is asleep.	✓ ✓ ✓
'Wake up, Bill,'	✓ ✓ ✓
said Peter.	✓ ✓
Sally is asleep.	✓ ✓ ✓
'Wake up, Sally,'	✓ ✓ ✓
said Mother.	✓ ✓
Father is shaving.	✓ ✓ ✓

2   Record a wrong response with the text under it.

> *Child:*   *home*
> Text: house   [One error]

3   If a child tries several times to read a word, record all his trials.

Child:	*here*	*h—*	*home*
Text:	house		

[One error]

Child:	*h—*	*ho—*	✓
Text:	home		

[No error]

Note that in both examples the child was judged to be solving the word, and not correcting an error.

4 If a child succeeds in correcting a previous error this is recorded as 'self-correction' (written SC).

Child:	where	when	SC	
Text:	were			[No error]

5 If no response is given to a word it is recorded with a dash. Insertion of a word is recorded over a dash.

No response   Insertion

Child:	—	Child:	here	
Text:	house	Text:	—	[In each case one error]

For contractions see page 23, 11C.

6 If the child baulks, unable to proceed a) because he is aware he has made an error and cannot correct it, or b) because he cannot attempt the next word, he is told the word (written as T). This preserves the storyline and starts the reader off again. (Wait no more than about three seconds.)

Child:	home		—		
Text:	house	T	house	T	[One error]

7 A verbal appeal for help (A) from the child is turned back to the child for further effort. Say '*You* try it' (recorded as Y). The response from the teacher is **not** a teaching interaction; it involves no prompting but is merely a shift of the initiative.

Child:	—	A		✓	✓	
Text:	house		Y			[One error]

8 Sometimes the child gets into a state of confusion and it is necessary to extricate him. The most detached method of doing this is to say 'Try that again', marking TTA on the record. This would not involve any teaching, but the teacher needs to indicate where the child should begin again. Put square brackets around the first set of muddled behaviour, enter the TTA, remember to count that as one error only (see page 22), and then begin a fresh record of the problem text. An example of this recording is at the top of the next page.

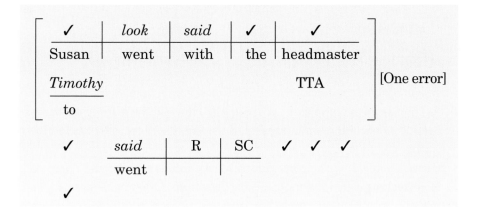

9 Repetition (R) is not counted as error behaviour. Sometimes it is used to confirm a previous attempt. Often it results in self-correction. It is useful to record this behaviour as it often indicates how much sorting out the child is doing. R, standing for repetition, is used to indicate repetition of a word, with R_2 or R_3 indicating the number of repetitions. If the child goes back over a group of words, or returns to the beginning of the line or sentence in his repetition, the point to which he returns is shown by an arrow.

Child:	*Here is the home*	R	SC
Text:	Here is the house		[No error]

10 Sometimes the child rereads the text (repetition) and corrects some but not all errors. The following example shows the recording of this behaviour.

Child:	*a*	SC	*house*	R	[One error
Text:	the		home		One SC]

11 If a child spells or sounds out the letters of a word, record capitals for spelling (as in HELP) and record letter or cluster breaks (as in h-e-l-p-ing) for sounding out.

12 Directional attack on the printed text is recorded by telling the child to 'Read it with your finger.' Sometimes you may notice signs that tell you the young reader is not following the directional rules for attending to print. To check on this select a few lines of print during the reading and say to the child, 'Read it with your finger.'

A brief observation will often be sufficient but extend the observation if you need to understand more about this behaviour. Even if teachers do not find pointing a desirable teaching prompt, they will still need to use it to collect some evidence of starting points, direction of scanning, and lapses or confusions from beginning readers.

Left to right	L → R	Snaking	⟵⟍	
Right to left	L ← R	Bottom to top	↑	

13   As soon as the reading ends, ask yourself, 'How did the reading of that text sound?' Add a comment at the end of the Running Record (see below).

14   Other behaviours. The conventions for recording and scoring relate only to correct responses, errors, and self-corrections. Other behaviours include pausing, sounding out the letters, and splitting words into parts. Research evidence has shown that teachers' records of such behaviours are much less reliable and cannot be included in the count or analysis.

A Running Record from a child who is making many errors is hard to record and score but the rule is to record as much of the behaviour as you can, and analyse objectively what is recorded.

How the reading sounds

Describe the reading behaviour recorded; it is important to listen closely to the reading as it occurs, since it provides information about the child's current literacy learning. Immediately following the reading and before you begin to analyse the detail of the record, write a few lines on what you just observed, your intuitive summation of the child's reading. This should be an overall reaction.

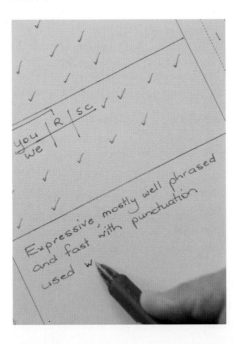

Comment on what the reader did well.

*   Was the text read at a good pace, or was it slow, or too fast?
*   Was he reading groups of words together in a phrased way?
*   Did the child's intonation and expression indicate understanding of the text?
*   Attend particularly to change over previous readings.

Assessment and comprehension

Running Records should be valued because they adhere to good assessment practices. Some teachers wish to add retelling or comprehension questions to the taking of a Running Record. Here are some comments and cautions.

- Comprehension is very dependent upon the difficulty level of the text. It makes no sense to assess comprehension on a hard text, nor on an easy text. If the text is at an appropriate instructional level for the child, then that tells the teacher she can expect and teach for understanding.
- Because different teachers ask different questions, their comprehension questions provide an unreliable gauge of a child's understanding of text.
- Research suggests the answers to comprehension questions depend more upon the difficulty of the sentence structure of the question than on the child's reading.

The reliability and validity of these assessments are not improved when teachers cannot agree on the scoring or when what teachers do is non-standard, like asking questions which differ in content, form or purpose.

Conversation about the story after taking Running Records adds to the teacher's understanding of the reader in useful ways, and leads the child into discourse about stories.

A record before scoring

The page from Paul's reading could have been made on a blank piece of paper. It shows 55 running words, and was only the first part of the Running Record that was taken. The scoring of errors (E) and self-corrections (SC) on the right-hand side is discussed on pages 21–23. Reread the text to yourself as you think the child read it.

Paul's record

Page of text	Running Record	E	SC
		Count	
The milk ran	✓ ✓ ✓		
all over the ground.	✓ ✓ ✓ g – / ground | garden |		
And there was the woman	✓ threw / there | th – | th – / T | ✓ ✓ R ✓ R₂		
with the magpie's tail in her hand.	✓ ✓ ✓ ✓ ✓ ✓		
"Woman, give me back my tail!"	W – / Woman | R₄ | ✓ g – / give | get | go ✓ ✓ ✓		
cried the magpie.	✓ ✓ ✓		
"I'll pin it on and fly back	✓ put / pin | pull | ✓ ✓ R the / and | R | SC ✓ ✓		
to my mother and father.	✓ ✓ ✓ ✓ ✓		
If you don't give me back my tail	✓ ✓ ✓ ✓ ✓ ✓ ✓		
I'll eat the cabbages in your garden."	✓ ✓ ✓ c – / cabbages | cabbage | R ✓ ✓ ✓		

The teacher made this summary:

Generally used meaning at challenging words and often used structure. When approximating he usually checked further, often by rereading, and this sometimes led to self-corrections. Approximations show that he is mainly using initial letters and is not searching further. He read with phrasing and retold the story confidently.

Scoring of errors and self-corrections

Review the Running Records of the child's behaviour on the book(s) you have selected and consider what was happening as the child read. Consider each error only up to and including the error (not the unread text).

Conventions for scoring

In counting the numbers of errors, some judgements must be made but the following have been found workable.

1   Credit the child with any correct or corrected words.

Child:	to	the	shops	
Text:	for	the	bread	
Score:	✗	✓	✗	[Two errors]

2   There is no penalty for trials which are eventually correct.

A
Child:	want	won't	SC
Text:	went		
Score:	—	—	✓

$\begin{bmatrix} \text{No error} \\ \text{One SC} \end{bmatrix}$

B
Child:	where	we	when	SC
Text:	were			
Score:	—	—	—	✓

$\begin{bmatrix} \text{No error} \\ \text{One SC} \end{bmatrix}$

C
Child:	f –	fet	✓
Text:	fright		
Score:	—	—	✓

[No error]

In example C the reader made two attempts to solve the word 'fright', the teacher wrote 'fet' as the best way she could record what she thought he said and then the child reached a solution. This is considered to be solving behaviour and there was no substitution of a word.

3   Insertions add errors so that a child can have more errors than there are words in a line.

Child:	*The*	*train*	*went*	*toot,*	*toot,*	*toot*	
Text:	The	little	engine	sighed	—	—	
Score:	✓	×	×	×	×	×	[Five errors]

4   However, the child cannot receive a minus score for a page. The lowest page score is 0.

5   Omissions. If a word, line or sentence is omitted each word is counted as an error. If pages are omitted (perhaps because two pages were turned together) they are not counted as errors. Note that in this case, the number of words on the omitted pages must be deducted from the Running Words Total before calculation.

6   Repeated errors. If the child makes an error (for example 'run' for 'ran') and then substitutes this word repeatedly, it counts as an error every time; but substitution of a proper noun (for example 'Mary' for 'Molly' or 'taxis' for 'Texas') is counted only the first time (even though various alternate substitutions are made).

7   Multiple errors and self-correction. If a child makes two or more errors (for example reads a phrase wrongly) each word is an error. If he then corrects all these errors each corrected word is a self-correction.

8   a) Broken words. Where a word is pronounced as two words (for example a/way) even when this is backed up by pointing as if it were two words, this is regarded as an error of pronunciation not as a reading error, unless what is said is matched to a different word.
b) Childish pronunciations such as 'pitcher' for 'picture' and 'gonna' for 'going to' are counted as correct.

9   Inventions defeat the system. When the young child is creatively producing his own version of the story the scoring system finally breaks down and the judgement 'inventing' is recorded for that page, story or book.

10   'Try that again.' When the child is in a tangle this instruction, which does not involve teaching, can be given. It counts as one error and only the second attempt is scored (see page 16).

11 Fewest errors. If there are alternative ways of scoring responses a general principle is to choose the method that gives the fewest possible errors as in **B** below.

A	*Child:*	*We*	*went*	*for*	*the*	*bread*				
	Text:	You	went	to	the	shop	for	the	bread	
	Score:	✗	✓	✗	✓	✗	✗	✗	✗	[Six errors]

B	*Child:*	*We*	*went*				*for*	*the*	*bread*	
	Text:	You	went	to	the	shop	for	the	bread	
	Score:	✗	✓	✗	✗	✗	✓	✓	✓	[Four errors]

C Sometimes contractions need to be dealt with under the fewest errors rule. When the reader says 'I'm' for 'I am' or 'dog is' for 'dog's' the fewest errors rule would score the word correct and the contraction part would count as one error.

Quantifying a Running Record

5

Step 1

Count the Running Words
150

Step 2

Ratio of Errors to Running Words
$\dfrac{\text{Errors}}{\text{Running Words}}$
$\dfrac{15}{150}$
1 : 10
One in ten

Step 3

Accuracy Rate
$100 - \dfrac{E}{RW} \times \dfrac{100}{1}$
$100 - \dfrac{15}{150} \times \dfrac{100}{1}$
= 90%

Step 4

Self-correction Ratio
$\dfrac{SC}{E + SC}$
$\dfrac{5}{15 + 5}$
1 : 4
One in four

The four boxes on the left provide the calculations corresponding to the steps outlined below. The conversion table provides quick access to accuracy rates.

Step 1: Count the words in the text, omitting titles.
Step 2: Count the errors, and enter the Error Ratio.
Step 3: Use the conversion table to find the Accuracy Rate.
Step 4: Work out the Self-correction Ratio.

Here is one way to think about self-corrections. There were 15 errors in 150 running words of text and the five self-corrections represent an extra five potential errors. Altogether the child made five self-corrections in 20 chances to self-correct.

Conversion Table

Error Ratio	Percent Accuracy	
1:200	99.5	
1:100	99	
1:50	98	
1:35	97	
1:25	96	Good opportunities for teachers to observe children's processing of texts
1:20	95	
1:17	94	
1:14	93	
1:12.5	92	
1:11.75	91	
1:10	90	
1:9	89	
1:8	87.5	
1:7	85.5	
1:6	83	The reader tends to lose the support of the meaning of the text
1:5	80	
1:4	75	
1:3	66	
1:2	50	

Turn back to page 20 and score that Running Record. Put one count in the error column for every error and one count in the self-correction column for every self-correction. Total each column and work out the Error Ratio, the Accuracy Rate, and the Self-correction Ratio.

Records for two competent readers

The next two examples capture the reading behaviours of two competent readers and provide the teacher with opportunities to read back from the record what Emma and Claire did. The records are used to introduce an analysis of how the text was read in the next chapter, Interpreting a Running Record.

Emma read well. There were no self-corrections to analyse on this page of her Running Record but her two errors allowed her teacher to identify one or two things to talk about. The teacher could talk about the omission of 'as', how what she said sounded right but differed from what the author wrote. Important? Perhaps not. A second discussion might be about how she could work more effectively on the information in the middle of unfamiliar words, which may well be a crucial change in processing which she needs to make.

Emma's record

Analysis of Errors and Self-corrections

Page of Text	Running Record	Information used E			SC		
		M	S	V	M	S	V
… resting their elbows on it, and talking over its	✓ ✓ ✓ ✓ ✓ ✓ ✓						
head. "Very uncomfortable for the Dormouse,"	✓. ✓ ✓ ✓ ✓						
thought Alice; "only as it's asleep, I suppose it	✓ ✓ ✓ —/as ✓ ✓ ✓ ✓						
doesn't mind."	✓ ✓.						
The table was a large one, but the three were all	✓ ✓ ✓ ✓ ✓ ✓ ✓ ✓ ✓						
crowded together at one corner of it. "No room!	✓ ✓ ✓ ✓ ✓ ✓. ✓ ✓						
No room!" they cried out when they saw Alice	✓ ✓ ✓ ✓ ✓ ✓ ✓						
coming. "There's plenty of room!" said Alice	✓. ✓ ✓ ✓ ✓ ✓						
indignantly, and she sat down in a large arm-chair	indently/indignantly ✓ ✓ ✓ ✓ ✓ ✓	M	(S)	(V)			
at one end of the table.	✓ ✓ ✓ ✓ ✓ ✓.						

Although 'indently' is an invented word, the 'in——ly' clearly fits a common way of creating an adverb in English; it is a structural feature of the language.

Claire made a number of errors on this text but she often self-corrected without any assistance. (Only a part of the record is shown and I simplified it.)

Claire's record

Page of Text	Running Record	Information used — E (M S V)	Information used — SC (M S V)
"Because I'm years older," Hannah smirked.	✓ ✓ ✓ ✓ R ✓ ✓.		
He gave up arguing and stomped off towards his	✓ ✓ ✓ ✓ ✓ ✓ ✓ ✓		
room. "See you in the morning," he said to	bedroom / room She|See SC ✓ ✓ ✓ ✓ ✓ ✓	Ⓜ Ⓢ Ⓥ / Ⓜ Ⓢ Ⓥ	M S Ⓥ
his mother to emphasize that he was ignoring	✓ ✓ and / to SC emphases / emphasize ✓ R ✓ ✓ ✓	Ⓜ Ⓢ V / M S Ⓥ	M S Ⓥ
Hannah.	Anna / Hannah SC .	Ⓜ Ⓢ Ⓥ	M S Ⓥ
He posed in front of his bedroom mirror. If	✓ possed / posed ✓ ✓ ✓ ✓ ✓. ✓	M Ⓢ Ⓥ	
Hannah was a damsel in distress, she couldn't	✓ ✓ ✓ ✓ ✓ district / distress SC ✓ ✓	M S Ⓥ	M Ⓢ Ⓥ
expect him to come galloping to her rescue.	✓ ✓ ✓ ✓ ✓ ✓ ✓.		
She could stay tied to the stake. He would	✓ ✓ ✓ died / tied SC ✓ ✓ ✓. ✓ ✓	M S Ⓥ	M Ⓢ Ⓥ
charge in cutting this way and that with his	✓ ✓ ✓ the / this ✓ ✓ ✓ ✓	M Ⓢ Ⓥ	
fearsome sword. All would fall before him and	✓ s...word / sword. ✓ ✓ ✓ ✓ ✓ ✓		
he would fight his way to where she was tied	✓ ✓ ✓ ✓ ✓ ✓ ✓ ✓		
and then …	✓ ✓ …		

Her teacher summarised the analysis of the reading like this:

Claire is constructing meaningful sentences and is using structure and visual information. She self-corrects most of her errors by picking up more visual information, and attempts all words. In her substitutions she is often using only visual information.

6

Interpreting a Running Record

There is another level of analysis that will help teachers to work out what information in the text the reader is attending to. To do this you must give closer attention to analysing the error and self-correction behaviours. The analysis takes a little time but it can uncover some important things about how the child is processing print (see pages 30–31).

Readers of text appear to make decisions about the quality of the message they are getting. One kind of theory would say the child is recalling words and attacking words; another kind of theory would say that the child is using information of various kinds to make a choice among possible responses. He is trying to get the best fit with the limited knowledge he has. *It is this second kind of theory that guides the following discussion.*

Think about the errors in the record

It is important to analyse every error to identify the kinds of information used. Look only at the sentence up to the error. Ask yourself, 'What led the child to do or say that?' For every error, ask yourself at least three questions:

> **Meaning (M)** Did the meaning or the messages of the text influence the error? Perhaps the reader brought a different meaning to the author's text.

> **Structure (S)** Did the structure (syntax) of the sentence up to the error influence the response? If the error occurs on the first word of the sentence, it is marked as positive for structure if the new sentence could have started that way.

> **Visual information (V)** Did visual information from the print influence *any part* of the error: letter, cluster or word?
> (See page 30 for more explanation of the 'V' for visual information category.)

Where an error is made, write the letters M (meaning), S (structure), V (visual information) in the error column. Circle the appropriate letter if the child's error showed that he could have been led by meaning, language structure, or visual information (which will include letter form and/or letter-sound relationships) from the sentence so far. You will probably be circling more than one kind of information. Do this for all errors even where they have been self-corrected. This first attempt is important.

Scan the record to answer two other questions

- Did the child's oral language produce the error, with little influence from the print?
- Was the child clearly getting some phonemic information from the printed letters? What makes you suspect this?

These two questions cannot be used in scoring a record because teachers cannot agree upon their interpretations, and the information is therefore unreliable. However, if the reader sometimes responds as if he were 'just talking', or if specific phonemic information is used, then certainly teachers can note these things in their records but do not need to include them in the formal summation of text reading.

Next, think about the self-corrections

Often readers make errors and without any prompting, work on the text in some way and self-correct the errors. It is as if they had a feeling that something was not quite right. Ask yourself, 'What led the child to do this?'

Where a self-correction has occurred, write the letters in the self-correction column and circle the appropriate one to record whether the extra information the reader used was meaning and/or structure and/or visual information. Examine each self-correction carefully. The corrected response will fit with all three sources of information but it is not helpful to automatically circle all three, as this will not indicate what led the child to make the self-correction.

Consider the pattern of responses

Now look at the overall pattern of the responses you have circled. Look for patterns in the circling and bring your analysis of errors and self-corrections together into a written summary. (It is important to look at what happens across the entire record because a single error or self-correction could have been unusual or accidental for the reader.)

Write your analysis of the pattern indicated in the child's use of the different kinds of information at the top of the Running Record next to the appropriate level of the text. This statement about the sources of information used and neglected, and *whether they were used together*, is essential to guide your subsequent teaching.

A completed Running Record sheet is on the next page. Note the following.

- Analysis of the use of meaning and structure and visual information is of little value unless it is done carefully.
- Consider the sentence only up to the error (not the unread text).
- Do not try to analyse omissions and insertions.
- The pattern of responses is merely a guide to what information is neglected, what is made a priority, and when the reader can combine the processing of different kinds of information.
- Avoid analyses for which you have no theoretical support.
- Always write a statement about how the reading sounded at the end of the record.

RUNNING RECORD SHEET

Name: __Sam__   Date: _____   D. of B.: _____   Age: __5__ yrs __9__ mths

School: __Westleigh__   Recorder: __C.B.__

Text Titles	Errors / Running Words	Error Ratio	Accuracy Rate	Self-correction Ratio
Easy _____	_____	1: _____	_____ %	1: _____
Instructional __Dogs (Highgate/P.M.) (seen)__	$\frac{3}{34}$	1: __11.3__	__91__ %	1: __2__
Hard _____	_____	1: _____	_____ %	1: _____

Directional movement ____✓____

Analysis of Errors and Self-corrections
Information used or neglected [Meaning (M), Structure or Syntax (S), Visual (V)]

Easy _____

Instructional __Meaning and structure are used predominantly for substitutions with some attention to visual information. Repetition and more visual information led to three self-corrections.__

Hard _____

Cross-checking on information (Note that this behaviour changes over time)

Meaning and structure cross-checked with visual information $\frac{dogs}{like}$ $\frac{little}{small}$ Count

Analysis of Errors and Self-corrections

Page	Title: Dogs	E	SC	E MSV	SC MSV
2	$\frac{s-}{Some}$ T ✓ ✓ ✓	I		M S (V)	
3	✓ ✓ ✓ ✓				
4	✓ ✓ ✓ $\frac{scary}{growly}$	I		(M)(S) V	
5	✓ $\frac{dogs}{like}$ R SC ✓ ✓		I	(M)(S) V	M S (V)
6	✓ ✓ ✓ ✓				
7	✓ ✓ ✓ $\frac{little}{small}$ R SC		I	(M)(S) V	M S (V)
8	✓ ✓ $\frac{dog\ is}{dog's}$ R SC ✓ ✓		I	(M)(S)(V)	M S (V)
	✓ ✓ $\frac{biggest}{cuddliest}$ R A T ✓ ✓	I		(M)(S) V	
	Read slowly with some intonation.				

29

7

Processing the information in print

When teachers ask themselves 'What does my record tell me?' they bring their own beliefs about literacy (their personal theory of literacy learning) and their background of professional experience to the task. Interpretations of Running Records are heavily weighted with the theoretical view the teacher already holds. My interpretations fit with my theory that progress depends on an increasing complexity in processing which enables the reader to read more difficult texts. I think of the child as working with several different types of knowledge about print (which I call different kinds of information).

To explain an error, consider what might have led the child up to the point of the error. To explain a self-correction, consider what kind of information might have led the child to spontaneously correct the error.

When teachers have different theories about what is important for the beginning reader to learn, they could interpret the same behaviour record in different ways. They may ask quite different questions of the data because they emphasise the importance of different things. Extensive research into what young readers do as they read text, and careful training of teachers as observers, ensure that behavioural records will look the same even though teacher interpretations might differ.

For example, examine the attention given in these analyses to 'V' standing for the visual information in print. During acquisition of literacy learning the visual information becomes intricately linked to phonemic information (the sounds of speech or phonology) so that children could probably be said to 'hear' a letter or cluster of letters they are looking at. Theorists tell us that visual information also links directly to a vocabulary of known words (spelling patterns or orthography). So, theoretically, the symbol V in the analysis of Running Records stands for the stimulus information on the page of print irrespective of whether the processing is through a phonological system or a visual system. This is a point at which teachers might differ in their understanding of what a reader was doing.

What if a reliable behavioural record does not support our expectations? Unable to deny that the actual behaviour did occur, we probably need to adjust any of our assumptions that are not supported by recorded data. So it is important that we have reliable records.

Running Records are useful if we remember the following things.

- Record error behaviour in full as the information is needed when interpreting the records.
- Poor observation will reduce the number of errors and inflate the accuracy score.
- Reliability drops as accuracy levels fall because there is more error to be recorded.
- Observation of poor readers is difficult and rigorous training is required to reach agreement on scoring because of the complexity of the error behaviour.
- The most reliable records would be obtained by scoring an observation immediately following its manual recording but for classroom teachers that is not usually possible.

Older readers: different signs of progress

If Running Records are used with older readers, *there should be a special reason for taking them.* They are excellent for recording the early phases of literacy acquisition but before long, what the reader is doing becomes too fast and too sophisticated for teachers to observe in real time. Literacy processing shifts gradually towards this.

Some of the changes to look for in older readers are these.

- It is an important sign of progress when errors contain several kinds of correct information even though the final decision is not quite correct. As the reader learns to process more information more quickly, behaviours change and new things can be noted. Errors occur even though the reader clearly used meaning and structure and visual information to get to a response (for example, *strong* for *sturdy*).
- Another change occurs when more proficient readers utter only the word beginning and then give the whole word. These are examples
  wu/would   pl/play   Pe/Peter   bu/but
- A similar kind of thing happens when the older reader corrects what might have been an error before giving the whole word, as in
  m…/parents   gar…/ground   d…/tied
- Sometimes there is more repetition as the older reader tries to regroup words in phrases.
- With older readers, self-correction occurs less frequently. Theoretically, we suppose that it has 'gone underground' and the reader is correcting errors before saying them. If the teacher introduces a more challenging text, the process of self-correcting may reappear. Even adults reading aloud can be heard to self-correct.

Records of individual and group progress

Education is primarily concerned with change in the learning of individual students, yet educators rarely document change over time in individuals as they learn. It is not difficult to collect evidence of change over time in early literacy learning, particularly from young children at the beginning of formal education.

Three ways of using Running Records to capture individual progress over time are shown.

Rochelle's progress at two observation points

Book Level	Progress
1	
2	
3	
4	
5	**Time 1 (date)**
6	*The Escalator* (easy)
7	*Going to School* (instructional)
8	*Playtime* (hard)
9	
10	
11	
12	**Time 2 (date)**
13	*The Pet Show* (easy)
14	*A Wet Morning* (instructional)
15	*Hungry Lambs* (hard)
16	
17	
18	

- In Rochelle's case, the teacher grouped the books that her class read into approximate levels of difficulty and placed numbers for these levels at the left side of her sheet. Then she took Running Records of Rochelle's reading of previously read texts on two occasions several months apart, and entered the names of the books Rochelle found easy, instructional or hard. Rochelle's progress is clear.

- A different record was used by a teacher who was keeping a close watch on Joan's progress by monitoring it frequently. This teacher used the Change Over Time in Text Level sheet (page 45) and entered the date of the observation along the horizontal line. She chose to take a record once a week of the reading of the current book after Joan had read it at least once (seen text). She entered an open circle for the instructional level of text read, because no story at a higher level of text reached the 90 percent accuracy criterion. The next week Joan raised the text difficulty level and the accuracy on what she had read fell below 90 percent, so she used a black circle on her graph. After two more weeks of teaching she raised the difficulty level again. (Meanwhile Joan read several new texts but all at the same level of difficulty.) From then onwards, as the teacher raised the text difficulty, Joan was able to meet the challenge except for once after a holiday break.

- A teacher can follow several different children, using the same plotting procedures. There are problems of clustering if the children are homogeneous in their progress. Graphs of progress made for a group of children will show individual differences in starting levels, in paths of progress, in fast or slow take-off and in final outcome levels. The teacher would be able to quickly identify any children who are reading material that is too difficult, preventing them from working in the context of mostly correct reading, or children who temporarily needed more of her attention. This is one way to monitor the progress of a group.

A weekly record of Joan's progress

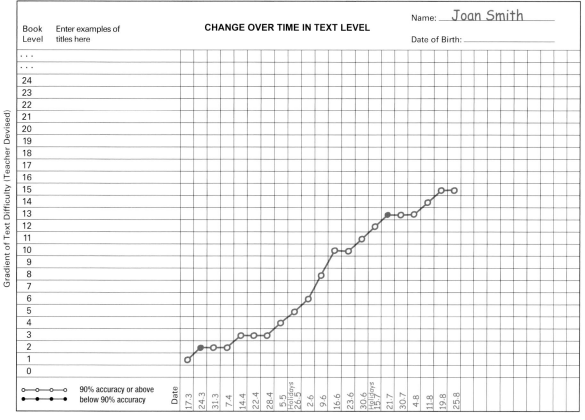

Teachers may follow the progress of several children

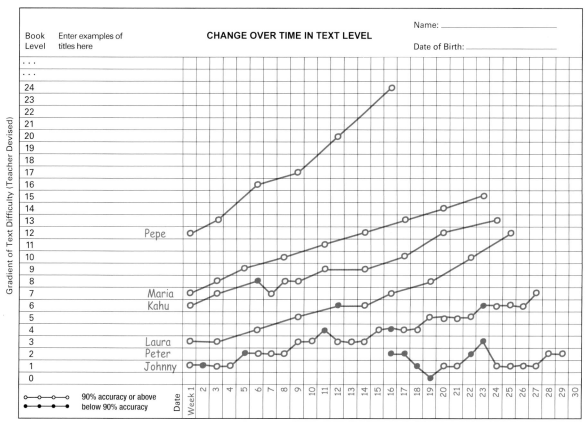

A different way to keep a record of progress is shown below. A child's progress through a series of reading book levels was listed from first to last along some gradient of difficulty and the accuracy with which each book was read was recorded. Day by day or week by week, a child's increasing control over text reading is captured on this record. It is reassuring to know that progress is being made as time passes. When that kind of record is also backed by an analysis of the literacy processing behaviours of the reader from time to time, teachers in classrooms and early intervention teachers have a tool for monitoring changes in how the reader works on the text, what the reader is noticing, what is easy, what is confusing, and what needs the teacher's attention.

An individual record of books read over 18 weeks

Week	Book title (publisher series)	Level	Accuracy	Rating	Self-correction ratio
1	*Nick's Glasses* (Ready to Read)	10	98%	Easy	1:1.3
2	*Breakfast* (Young Shorty)	12	94%	Inst.	1:2.5
3	*Mark Fox* (Young Shorty)	14	96%	Easy	1:2
4	*The Hat Trick* (Bangers & Mash)	13	98%	Easy	1:1
5	*Burglars* (Young Shorty)	15	93%	Inst.	1:2
6	*Burglars* (Young Shorty)	15	96%	Easy	1:1.3
7	*Wet Days at School* (City Kids)	14	98%	Easy	1:2
8	*Buster is Lost* (Lang. in Action)	15	94%	Inst.	1:2
9	*My Ghost* (Mount Gravatt)	15	95%	Easy	1:2
10	*A Hat for Pedro* (Pedro Books)	14	95%	Easy	1:1.5
11	*Pedro and the Cars* (Pedro Books)	15	90%	Inst.	1:3
12	*Monster Looks for a Friend* (Monster Books)	16	98%	Easy	1:1.3
13	*Pot of Gold* (Scott Foresman)	16	96%	Easy	1:1.5
14	*Giant's Hiccups* (Open Highways)	17	96%	Easy	1:2
15	*Monster and the Magic Umbrella* (Monster Books)	18	97%	Easy	1:1.3
16	*Chocolate Shop* (Young Shorty)	18	94%	Inst.	1:2
17	*Beauty and the Bus* (Hart-Davis)	18	94%	Inst.	1:2
18	*Magpie's Tail* (Ready to Read)	19	98%	Easy	1:2

8

Suggestions for using Running Records in classroom settings

School entry checks

Teachers will have their own ways of collecting and recording information about learners from the time they enter school. Running Records can be taken on children's earliest attempts to read little books, enriching the teacher's observations.

Education systems tend to be highly selective about what they use for a baseline assessment of early literacy learning. Instead of limiting observations to a measure of letter knowledge, teachers could use a range of tasks because they would be more likely to capture the areas that reveal the strengths of individual children. Running Records might be part of such a broad-ranging assessment for particular children.

For teaching individuals

Using the Running Record for teaching purposes, teachers might

- first try to find a book level appropriate for a child, then try an easier book and a harder book
- check a child's progress after individual instruction
- evaluate whether a lift in text level is appropriate
- observe particular difficulties in individual children in order to modify instructional emphases
- monitor progress in order to place a child in an appropriate instructional group or class
- build a cumulative record of an individual's progress over time.

For teaching groups

Using Running Records to inform group instruction, teachers might

- group children who could work together
- evaluate progress and see when regrouping is desirable
- see how different the processing of particular children is, and
- give attention to an individual learner at the time of the group instruction.

Running Records may be used to capture the oral reading behaviour of older readers (see page 31) when there is a particular purpose for observing this (Johnston, 1997, 2000).

Evidence of what is being emphasised in the classroom

If teachers take records of text reading with a wide sample of children, they will quickly discover which things are fostered by the classroom instruction.

Evidence of good outcomes may be observed. For example, most of the children may be

- getting it all together smoothly
- working on new words in ways that surprise and impress the teacher
- enjoying the stories and discussing features of those stories
- showing improved control over structure in phrased reading.

On the other hand teachers may observe

- word-by-word reading
- sounding out words in single phonemes
- not attending to meaning and reading nonsense
- ignoring first letters or not going beyond these
- not attending to detail in the middle of a word.

If any of these behaviours persist, they may indicate a problem for a particular group of learners.

If the programme is changed so that new emphases are introduced, like a shift to asking for more fluent, phrased reading, or teaching readers how to approach multisyllabic words with several unstressed vowels, then Running Records can be used to monitor whether the changes that are made to instruction are having the desired effect. Running Records can help teachers improve the reading of individuals, but they can also be used for planning and monitoring shifts in the instruction delivered in classrooms.

9

A theory of literacy processing

All readers, whether they are beginners working on their first books or effective adult readers, need to find and use different kinds of information in print. They combine the information they find with what they carry in their heads from their past experiences with language. Any correct word fits a matrix of relationships like a piece in a jigsaw puzzle. That is what text is, a sequence of relationships all of which fit.

Most children engage with books at the level of the story, not with isolated words. Children like to read stories and they learn a great deal about print and text as they do this. After only one year of instruction, the high-progress readers can pull together information from the meanings of words, phrases, sentences and texts, along with his knowledge of language structure and information from the print.

Children who have many abilities and a fair grasp of letters and words may still find it hard to pull this information *together* when they are moving across lines of continuous text.

There are two sides to this challenge. On the one hand, the child must sort out what to attend to on the page of print and in what order to use which pieces of information (*awareness and integration*).

On the other hand, he has to call up things he already knows from different parts of his brain to meet up with the new information in print he is looking at (*the integration of different kinds of information*).

During beginning reading, children give us overt signs about what they are attending to and what links they are making. Their behaviours provide signals that help teachers decide how best to lift their performance levels. For a short time, these signals provide teachers with opportunities to be very helpful. Over time reading becomes a very fast and silent process and there is little evidence of what the neural networks are doing.

Some of the processing changes teachers capture in their records include gaining control over directional movement, learning one-to-one matching of spoken to written words, becoming able to check on oneself, and noticing discrepancies. Self-correction follows from self-monitoring, searching and making all information match.

As a child gains control over these various ways of working with information in texts, he begins to build a literacy processing system that learns to extend itself. The child is learning to read because of the effective processing he does when he reads. This self-tutoring occurs at faster and faster rates under the control of sound self-monitoring and self-correcting systems.

Recommended reading

Clay, M.M. (2010). *The puzzling code.* Auckland, New Zealand: Pearson.

Clay, M.M. (2013). *An observation survey of early literacy achievement* (3rd ed.). Auckland, New Zealand: Heinemann.

Clay, M.M. (2014). *By different paths to common outcomes* (revised ed.). Auckland, New Zealand: The Marie Clay Literacy Trust.

Clay, M.M. (2015). *Becoming literate: The construction of inner control.* Auckland, New Zealand: The Marie Clay Literacy Trust.

Clay, M.M. (2016). *Literacy lessons designed for individuals* (2nd ed.). Auckland, New Zealand: The Marie Clay Literacy Trust.

Clay, M.M. (2017). *Concepts about print for classroom teachers.* Auckland, New Zealand: The Marie Clay Literacy Trust.

Johnston, P.J. (1997). *Knowing literacy: Constructive literacy assessment.* York, ME: Stenhouse.

Johnston, P.J. (2000). *Running Records: A self-tutoring guide.* Portland, ME: Stenhouse.

Recording sheets

RUNNING RECORD SHEET

Name _____ Date _____ D. of B. _____ Age _____ yrs _____ mths

School _____ Recorder _____

Text Titles	Errors Running Words	Error Ratio	Accuracy Rate	Self-correction Ratio
Easy	_____	1: _____	_____ %	1: _____
Instructional	_____	1: _____	_____ %	1: _____
Hard	_____	1: _____	_____ %	1: _____

Directional movement _____

Analysis of Errors and Self-corrections

Information used or neglected [Meaning (M), Structure or Syntax (S), Visual (V)]

Easy _____

Instructional _____

_____

Hard _____

_____

Cross-checking on information (Note that this behaviour changes over time)

		Count		Analysis of Errors and Self-corrections	
				Information used	
Page	Title	E	SC	E MSV	SC MSV

Page		Count		Analysis of Errors and Self-corrections	
				Information used	
		E	SC	E MSV	SC MSV
		E	SC	E MSV	SC MSV

CHANGE OVER TIME IN TEXT LEVEL

Name: _____

Date of Birth: _____

Gradient of Text Difficulty (Teacher Devised)

Book Level   Enter examples of titles here

Levels (top to bottom): . . . | . . . | 24 | 23 | 22 | 21 | 20 | 19 | 18 | 17 | 16 | 15 | 14 | 13 | 12 | 11 | 10 | 9 | 8 | 7 | 6 | 5 | 4 | 3 | 2 | 1 | 0

Date

● 90% accuracy or above

○ below 90% accuracy

Weekly Observations

Acknowledgements

The Marie Clay Literacy Trust acknowledges with thanks the teachers and children who are featured in the photographs in this book.

Running Records examples on page 8 reproduced with permission of C. Lyons.

Running Records example on page 14 reproduced with permission of D. Churchward.

The following text extracts and *Ready to Read* books are © The Crown, and used with permission.

Extract on page 6 from *The Wolf and the Seven Little Kids* (retold by Fran Hunia, illustrated by Nina Price) in *Horrakapotchkin!*, Wellington: Learning Media, 1991.

Examples on pages 20, 25 and 26 from *The Learner as a Reader*, Wellington: Learning Media, 2006.

Whitebait Season by Tracey Cormack, illustrated by Elspeth Alix Batt, Wellington: Learning Media, 2009.

The Stowaway by Katie Furze (no illustrator listed), in *Junior Journal 45*, Wellington: Ministry of Education, 2012.

Earmuffs by Susan Paris, illustrated by Kat Chadwick, Wellington: Ministry of Education, 2014.

Isobel's Garden by Maria Hansen, illustrated by Andrew Burdan, Wellington: Ministry of Education, 2014.

A Place to Sleep by Andrea Foot, illustrated by Fifi Colston, Wellington: Ministry of Education, 2014.